HERBERT READ

PAUL NASH

PENGUIN BOOKS

THE PENGUIN MODERN PAINTERS

Editor Sir Kenneth Clark

Made and Printed in Great Britain by Hunt, Barnard & Company, Ltd.
The Sign of the Dolphin, London and Aylesbury, Buckinghamshire
Colour Plates by John Swain & Son, Ltd.

Published by
Penguin Books Limited
Harmondsworth, Middlesex, England
1944

COLOUR PLATES

BLACK AND WHITE PLATES

Plate 2   FALLING STARS (1912), 16 × 12, *pen, wash and chalk*; owned by Sir William Rothenstein

Plate 4   THE MENIN ROAD (1918), 84 × 168, *oil*; owned by The Imperial War Museum

Plate 6   CHILTERNS UNDER SNOW (1923), 30 × 25, *oil*; owned by Mrs. Felce

Plate 8   DYMCHURCH STEPS (1923), 15½ × 22¾, *water-colour*; owned by Major G. Fairfax Harvey, M.C.

Plate 10   ST. PANCRAS LILIES (1927), 32 × 20, *oil*; owned by The Belfast Art Gallery

Plate 12   STILL LIFE (1927), 36 × 28, *oil*; owned by Richard Wyndham, Esq.

Plate 14   ATLANTIC (1931), 15 × 22, *water-colour*; owned by Miss Macaw

Plate 16   LANDSCAPE OF THE MEGALITHS (1934), 25 × 30, *oil*; owned by The Leicester Galleries

Plate 18   LANDSCAPE FROM A DREAM (1938), 40 × 30, *oil*; owned by The Contemporary Art Society

Plate 20   MONSTER FIELD (1939), 40 × 30, *oil*; owned by The Durban Art Gallery

Plate 22   EARTH HOME *or* THE FORTRESS (1939), 36 × 28, *oil*; owned by Charles Kearley, Esq.

Plate 24   MOONLIGHT VOYAGE: FLYING AGAINST GERMANY (1940), 31 × 22, *water-colour and chalk*;
owned by The Air Ministry

Plate 26   LEBENSRAUM (1939), 22½ × 15, *collage, water-colour and chalk, leaves, etc.*;
owned by Captain Maurice Cardiff

Plate 28   NORTHERN ADVENTURE (1929–41), 36 × 28, *oil*; owned by Mrs. Margaret Nash

Plate 30   MADAMITE MOON (1941), 22 × 15, *water-colour*; owned by The Redfern Gallery for the Artist

Plate 32   PILLAR AND MOON (1932–42), 30 × 20, *oil*; owned by The Tate Gallery

PAUL NASH

AFTER the passage of a quarter of a century, during which we have endured the obliterating experiences of two world wars, nothing is so difficult to reconstruct as the hopes and aspirations of an age ignorant of all that was in store for it. It was an age of peace and security, of complacency and priggishness: and a young man who decided to become an artist in such an atmosphere was faced by problems which are no longer real to us, and which, even if we could revive them in all their urgency, would seem merely futile. The artist whose work we are now going to consider was born in 1889. After an unsuccessful effort to train for the Navy, and a short but aimless period at St. Paul's School, he decided, in the year 1907, to become an artist, and went to the Chelsea Polytechnic to acquire the necessary skill. He sprang from a background which was typically English—the Navy, the Law,

the Land, a substantial house in Kensington, a country retreat in Buckinghamshire.

Whistler was dead: art in England was dormant. It was a world in which the sprightly academicism of Augustus John could excite . . . well, could excite. Ricketts and Shannon, Conder and the Rothensteins—these were the shimmering stars in a twilight through which the sinister figures of Oscar Wilde and Aubrey Beardsley still seemed to slouch. Walter Sickert was the closest link with reality—the reality of Degas and Manet, but Sickert was not then taken so seriously as of late. It may be a little out of proportion in an essay devoted to another artist, but I would like to quote a criticism of Sickert which George Moore wrote in that doldrum epoch: it will serve as well as anything to give us the atmosphere of the period.

"According to his æstheticism, any grey tint will do for the sky provided the paint is nicely laid on, and with brown and a little Indian red the roofs and the shadows can be achieved. His one preoccupation is beauty of touch, and he gets it in the curve of the pavement. He has invented a formula which leaves out almost everything, and is therefore suitable to his own talent and to the talents of a large following, principally ladies. For the last seven summers his pupils have been painting in our streets, and they have left London seeking gable ends in all the old English towns; they have spread over the continent; Dieppe has not a wall left unpainted; they have reached Venice, and St. Mark's affords endless opportunities for their art; they have gone on to Constantinople and to Egypt, applying their method unembarrassed by the fact that in Egypt the relations of the sky and earth are the reverse of what they are here. . . . But truth of effect does not trouble them. The strip of grey that sets off the tower in Smith's Square, Westminster, furnishes an equally truthful background for the domes and minarets of Egypt; and hundreds of small pictures of unvarying merit are brought back—faint designs in gold frames, inoffensive always, and sometimes soothing to the eye."[1]

George Moore was trying to persuade young English painters that it was not necessary to trail to that mecca of the art student—Julian's studio in Paris: they should rather stay in England and study "the naïve simplicity" of our own tradition. It is possible that Paul Nash heard this advice and took it to heart. He was, at any rate, to remain uncompromisingly English. He had a family link with Edward Lear, as English a genius as anyone could find, and he often, in the impressionable years, gazed at Lear's water-colours which hung on the walls in his aunt's house. But the artist's earliest efforts recall a simplicity still more naïve—the idyllic mysticism of Blake's wood-engravings. I do not think Paul Nash has ever lost that element—it is the substance of the charge that he is a literary painter, about which I shall have something to say presently.

The one revolutionary event in those pre-cataclysmic days was the Post-Impressionist Exhibition held at the Grafton Galleries from November, 1910, to January, 1911, followed and reinforced by a second and more extreme exhibition held in the same place in the following autumn. When the history of English art in the

[1] *Impressions and Opinions* ("Une Recontre au Salon").

early twentieth century comes to be written, a very interesting and very entertaining chapter will have to be devoted to the immediate reception and permanent effects of this demonstration —it was more than an exhibition: it was a campaign conducted with terrifying critical din. In a manifesto printed in the catalogue of the second exhibition Mr. Clive Bell could cry: "The battle is won. We all agree now that any form in which an artist can express himself is legitimate, and the more sensitive perceive that there are things worth expressing that could never have been expressed in traditional forms". It was in this year of excitement that Paul Nash himself was first introduced to the world, in a modest exhibition of landscape drawings and watercolours at the Carfax Gallery. The forms seemed traditional enough, but the discerning critic could perceive a quality in some of the drawings which, though in no way related to the Post-Impressionist Movement, was too imaginative to be included within the academic conventions. The discerning critic, at this time, happened to be William Rothenstein, who bought a drawing in chalk, pen and wash, called *The Falling Stars*, which, however jejune it may now appear in view of the artist's later development, deserves to be carefully considered as a revelation of the artist's original tendency. It shows two contorted pine-trees moulded in ghostly moonlight against a night sky, across which two falling stars trace their burning way. The technique is summary— no striving after "beauty of touch". It is the technique of Blake, an art of imagination and outline, of imagination given visual precision.

The Carfax Exhibition was a considerable success for a young and unknown artist. Nash was now invited to exhibit with the New English Art Club, and his work for a time took on a "New English" quality: that is to say, it became more precise, more objective, more decorative, more eclectic. A work like *The Elms*, of 1914, which is reproduced as plate 3, belongs to this phase, but still more representative is the *Summer Garden* of the same year: it is Chinese in its exotic delicacy, but very native in its primness.

If the world of Summer 1914 had not ended so dramatically, Paul Nash might have continued to paint pictures in the genteel idiom of the New English Art Club. But in September of that year he joined the Artist Rifles, was some time afterwards given a commission in the Hampshire

Regiment, and eventually saw active service in France. Invalided home in the summer of 1917, he held a small exhibition of drawings he had made in the trenches, and this aroused so much attention that he was made an official war artist and returned to the Front in October. He made a large number of sketches and notes, and these formed the basis of a series of water-colours, lithographs and oil-paintings which was exhibited at the Leicester Galleries in May, 1918. I had myself just returned from the Front, and it is perhaps worth recording that my interest in Paul Nash's work dates from this time. I was in no mood for any falsification of this theme: I wanted to see and hear the truth told about our hellish existence in the trenches. As I have recorded elsewhere,[1] I was immediately convinced by the pictures I then saw, "because here was someone who could convey, as no other artist, the phantasmagoric atmosphere of No Man's Land". Other artists were to depict the psychological horrors of war—especially the poets and novelists—but the aspect which Paul Nash revealed was the outrage on Nature—the

[1] *Paul Nash:* a Portfolio of Colour Plates with an Introduction by Herbert Read, London (Soho Gallery), 1937.

Nature which had been so delicate and sensuous to New English eyes. The revulsion which we had experienced could not have been more violent. Here, for example, are the feeble words in which I myself had tried to convey our outraged feelings: they come from a narrative which I was writing at the Front about the same time that Paul Nash was making his sketches:

"All was black and upriven. In the valley the shell-holes were full of water and reflected the harsh cold sky. Devil's Wood was a naked congregation of shattered trunks, like an old broken comb against the skyline. An emotion—a sudden realization and anger—flushed his brain. This was his earth, earth of lithe green trees, earth of vigorous sap and delicate growth. Now riven and violated: a wide glabrous desolation: a black diseased scab, erupted and pustulous . . .". Such words defeat their purpose, simply because the reader does not believe in their objectivity. But Paul Nash's pictures were, as I have said, immediately convincing. There was selection and formalization, as there must be in all art. But there was the direct communication of truth, and therefore of emotion. Our experience had been recorded—recorded for as long as our civilization cared to preserve the historical truth. Luckily this was generally recognized at the time, and before the war ended Paul Nash had been commissioned to paint important panels for the Imperial War Museum and the Canadian War Records. And meanwhile the artist himself had emerged from relative obscurity to the front rank of English painters.

I have described these war paintings as formalized. There was formal composition in the traditional sense, but there was also evidence that the experience of war had not altogether obliterated the experience of post-impressionism. The formalism tended towards certain simplifications and emphases of a geometrical nature which could only have their origins in the cubism of Picasso and Gris: perhaps also in the futurism of Boccioni and Severini. This cubist influence has persisted all through Paul Nash's development, but it was never stronger than in the period succeeding the war—a period which culminates in an exhibition held at the Leicester Galleries in 1924. Again one must try to re-create a mood— the mood of the artist suddenly released from the limitations and frustrations of war, facing the future in a spirit of new hope and aspiration. The realism of our experience had made us idealists at heart: we bounded forward with renewed confidence, founding magazines, organizing societies and exhibitions, relentlessly experimenting with new forms and techniques. Eliot's first poems had appeared, and Joyce's *Ulysses* was being serialized in the *Egoist*. For a time we were only too eager to forget the war—to bury our horrible memories. It was not until 1924 or 1925 that the war became a possible—or at any rate a popular—subject again. Meanwhile Paul Nash was casting round with restless energy for an appropriate activity. He began to design for the theatre and for textiles. (He was responsible for the scene and costumes in the fantasy Barrie wrote for Karsavina, which was produced with music by Bax in 1920; he also designed scenes and costumes for *A Midsummer Night's Dream* and *King Lear* in the Players' Shakespeare Series, edited by Granville Barker.) He found a sympathetic medium in wood-engraving and exploited his distinctive talent for book illustration (he illustrated the Nonesuch Press edition of *Genesis*, 1923—the first of a famous series of illustrated books—and made several drawings for T. E. Lawrence's *Seven Pillars of Wisdom*).

But all these activities were subordinate to the main business of painting, and it was in the oils and water-colours of this period that his more profound intuitions found expression.

I use the doubtful word "intuition" because what we are concerned with in the most distinctive work of Paul Nash must be called an intuition of the *genius loci*. That faculty of apprehension was already present in the war landscapes, though we do not willingly ascribe "genius" to that particular "locus". But now that the artist was in England again, in woods and valleys from which the evil spirits had long ago absconded, the faculty could work with more joyful effect, to reveal the immemorial values in the natural scene. The first landscapes after the war are still deliberately formalized. The pattern of drooping boughs and fan-shaped foliage is sophisticated: it is imposed on the natural facts, not emergent from them. But between the landscapes of 1919 or 1920, and the *Pond* or the *Chilterns Under Snow* of 1923, a significant change has taken place. The formal element is still emphatic, as it is in Cézanne, in all "intuitive" painters: there is still a trace of wilful arabesque: but in general the natural fact,

in a word the truth, is in control. This achievement is all the clearer in a series of paintings made at Dymchurch in Kent in the year 1923. Superficially, these are among the most formal and geometric of the artist's works. Nevertheless, the form is inherent in the scene—in the long, low level stretches of the beach, in the linear perspective of the sea-wall. Here were natural elements which lent themselves without distortion to the tendency towards abstraction which the post-impressionist movement had inherited from Cézanne. In so far as the abstraction was inherent in the scene it might be said that the artist's task was made easy for him: he could get his abstract effect without too much distortion. But the ease of this particular solution only served to make clear to the artist that success depended on the reconciliation of form and fact, and when, after this enlightening experience, he began to range over a vastly wider variety of scene, he still carried with him the secret of that success.

The succeeding four years were as experimental as any that went before, but the search was for subject rather than treatment. The period begins with a five-months' stay in the south of France, during which material was collected which was to last for many bleak days in England. It is a period of widening contrasts. By the beginning of 1927, the tendency to abstraction seems to have given way entirely to a free "painterly" style—almost to the æstheticism of "touch", "so soothing to the eye". The first still-lifes belong to this period, and again show a restless experimentation—from the Cézannish *Still-life* in the Richard Wyndham collection by way of the plastic *Dahlias* and *St. Pancras Lilies* to the autumnal *Swan Song* with its anticipations of a surrealist phase—all three paintings belonging to the same year, 1927. With the *Swan Song*—painted at Iden near Rye in Sussex—the way seems open to an imaginative freedom of treatment far removed from the artist's earlier style. But actually the geometric tendency was first to flare up again, and a series of still-lifes, of which the *Dead Spring* of 1928 is typical, was to intervene. At first sight these rigid architectural structures, in which instruments of precision sometimes make a symbolical appearance, are far removed from the irrational composition of *Swan Song*. But they can nevertheless be described as an attempt to carry the urge to abstraction into the realm of fantasy. The transit was successfully made in the drawings which Paul Nash made for the La Belle Sauvage edition of Sir Thomas Browne's *Urn Burial*, a book which will always be treasured, for it is one of the loveliest achievements of contemporary English art. In a drawing like *The Soul Visiting the Mansions of the Dead* Paul Nash evolved a completely original fantasy. It may seem to owe something to Chirico or Giacometti, but one has only to compare this drawing with the *Atlantic* which immediately precedes it to see that the fantasy actually emerges out of the objective observation of fact: and the ambivalence thus established was in effect a personal discovery of the essential truth which was at this time being advanced by the surréalistes in France—I mean their insistence on the contemporaneity of the rational and the irrational, of reality and the dream.

In the next few years Paul Nash was to travel a good deal, sometimes in search of health, sometimes for pleasure, and once, when he went to America in 1931 as member of the International Jury of Award at the Pittsburgh International Exhibition, *en mission*. In 1934 he spent a short time in Spain and Morocco, after a longer stay for medical treatment in Nice. But he was now too well launched on a voyage of imagination to be visibly affected by a change of terrestrial scene. He was now conscious of his course, of his artistic destiny. And it was a destiny which he felt to be peculiarly English. Early in this year, 1933, he had taken a leading part in the formation of a new group of English artists—painters, sculptors and architects—which adopted the name UNIT ONE. In a letter which appeared in *The Times* on June 2nd he announced the formation of the group in terms which were not only uncompromisingly nationalist, but included a definition of purpose which showed how consciously representative our artist had become:

"Only the most stubborn can dispute that English art has always suffered from one crippling weakness—the lack of structural purpose. With few exceptions our artists have painted 'by the light of Nature' . . . This immunity from the responsibility of design has become a tradition; we are frequently invited to admire the 'unconscious' beauties of the British School—'so faithful to Nature'. Nature we need not deny, but art, we are inclined to feel, should control.

"This precept is in danger of being forgotten. About every seven years English art goes back on her tracks. She has never forgotten that she invented Impressionism and Pre-Raphaelitism and, inevitably, she seeks to revive the favourite forms of expression. It may be observed that we are now heading for a new revival, either of one or both; in any case, the Nature cult in some form or other. Against this are opposed a few artists anxious to go forward from the point they have reached, instead of turning with the tide. The fact that some of them have come through many phases and arrived at a so-called abstract expression is not important; they have come through and wish to go on. This tends to isolate them from the majority of their contemporaries. They discover that what they stand for is decidedly at variance with the great Unconscious School of Painting; also, they seem to be lacking in reverence for Nature as such. These facts are frequently pointed out to them. Their answer is that they are interested in other matters which seem to them more engrossing, more immediate. Design, for instance—considered as a structural pursuit; imagination, explored apart from literature or metaphysics."

Most manifestoes are read with embarrassment ten years after their appearance, but this one by exception still rings true. The Unit itself was doomed to early disruption: the causes had little to do with the principles it professed. Three years later it looked as though it had been completely submerged under a wave which had been gathering weight and force outside our shores—surrealism. Paul Nash accepted an invitation to participate in the Surrealist Exhibition of 1936, where design, considered as a structural pursuit, seemed to be the remotest of objectives. For a year or two the English tradition was lost in a cauldron of excitement—premonitory of the international chaos that was to be let loose in September, 1939. How, it may be asked, could an artist who had so recently declared himself in favour of a structural purpose in art, and of an imagination free from metaphysics, now subscribe so openly to the apotheosis of unreason? To answer that question we must look a little closer at the terms involved in such an apparent contradiction.

I would say myself that there is no real contradiction between art, conceived as design, and the unconscious. The unconscious does, in fact, reveal design. Not only is the dream, when understood, a dramatic unity, but even in its plastic manifestations the unconscious possesses a principle of organization. This is too complicated a fact to demonstrate in an essay devoted to another subject, especially as the whole question is still incompletely explored and debatable. But it should be obvious that a declaration in favour of the structural principle does not necessarily exclude the intangible elements of the imagination. A painter so dedicated to the *genius loci* as Paul Nash was never likely to compromise this aspect of reality. He makes this very clear in some sentences devoted to English painting of the past which occur in a statement contributed to the joint manifesto of Unit One:[1]

"There seems to exist, behind the frank expressions of portrait and scene, an imprisoned spirit: yet this spirit is the source, the motive power which animates this art. These pictures are the vehicles of this spirit, but somehow they are inadequate, being only echoes and reflections of familiar images (in portrait and scene). If I were

[1] *Unit One: the Modern Movement in English Architecture, Painting and Sculpture.* Edited by Herbert Read. London (Cassell), 1934.

asked to describe this spirit I would say it is of the land; *genius loci* is, indeed, almost its conception. If its expression could be designated I would say it is almost entirely lyrical. . . . We, to-day, must find new symbols to express our reaction to environment. In some cases this will take the form of an abstract art; in others we may look for some different nature of imaginative research. But, in whatever form, it will be a subjective art."

And then, in a concluding paragraph, Paul Nash describes an experience and defines an attitude which fully anticipates any of the work which, during the next five years, was to be dubbed "surrealist":

"Last summer I walked in a field near Avebury where two rough monoliths stand up, sixteen feet high, miraculously patterned with black and orange lichen, remnants of an avenue of stones which led to the Great Circle. A mile away, a green pyramid casts a gigantic shadow. In the hedge, at hand, the white trumpet of a convolvulus turns from its spiral stem, following the sun. In my art I would solve such an equation."

The art of these five years, 1934 to 1938, succeeds in solving such equations. The natural organic fact, the present life of flower and leaf, invades the animistic landscape, the sacred habitation of familiar spirits. The shell, the fossil, the withered stalk, fungus, tree and cloud, are so many elements in a druidic ritual. The synthesis, the solution of the equation, is not literature: it is not metaphysics. It may be magic, but, if so, it is only reviving the first and most potent function of art.

These years had seen exhibition after exhibition, and full recognition in all the officially organized international events of the art world. Many public collections, at home and abroad, had acquired the artist's work, and it had indeed never been lacking in what might be called collector's appeal. At any time in the past fifteen years Paul Nash might have rested on his laurels, content with some arrested cliché of expression. That, indeed, is what the public likes, and only a few artists are sufficiently strong in will and inspiration to drive on in restless imaginative research. A new war came and Paul Nash was inevitably selected as one of the first official artists. New subjects served as so many new facets in which the development of his artistic vision was reflected. His first war work was done for the Air Ministry, but there could be no question of subordinating imagination to reportage. The wrecked airplane was one more monolithic object, fallen unexpectedly from the sky, but endowed with an additional mystery, ominous and deathly. A dump of wrecked German planes fell into the geometrical design first extricated from the sea at Dymchurch, twenty years before: but this time it was a Dead Sea, metallic waves harbouring no life, for ever devoid of movement. But soaring in the clouds the airplane is animated, becomes an immense sword-fish or vulture, alive with the electric voracity of animals that inhabit the extreme elements.

In the midst of this specialized work the normal activity of the artist's imagination has continued. New equations have been solved. The artist's environment is still his pre-occupation: landscape his favourite theme. The water-colour technique has grown more subtle, the touch of the brush feathery, the colours falling on the paper as gently as snowflakes. It is the English idiom, which the artist himself has described as "a pronounced linear method in design, no doubt traceable to sources in Celtic ornament, or to a predilection for the Gothic idiom. A peculiar bright delicacy in the choice of colours—somewhat cold, but radiant and sharp in key". Paul Nash has passed his fiftieth year, but his art shows no decline of imaginative invention or of technical efficiency. Though often interrupted by illness, he has worked with consistent devotion to his art, and the corpus of his work, in a wide range of traditional and experimental media, is impressive. It might be objected that the scale is seldom grandiose—a painting like *The Battle of Britain* (48×72) is exceptional. But the artist is often frustrated in this respect, for, however congenial to his talent and tempting to his ambition, the fact is that the grandiose in painting is not compatible with contemporary moods, nor with contemporary habits. Our expression is, as Paul Nash himself has said, "almost entirely lyrical".

I write, not as a painter, nor even as someone particularly knowledgeable about the technique of painting: I write as a poet, and that is perhaps why the art of Paul Nash has always had a special appeal for me. But it would be doing him a disservice if I allowed it to be assumed that this involves a limitation. Pictures are not made for painters, nor are poems written for poets, though a certain "mystery" belongs to every craft. The appeal of any art is to the total sensibility: to the senses as the instigators of mind and emotion. To say of a painter that he is poetic is to describe a quality, not of his art, but of his imagination.

The imagination is of many kinds, but "poesis" is its creative or structural aspect. Poetry is intuition, invention, the active aspect of imagination: poetry can be translated into words, or into sound, or into form and colour. Poetry is the original quality of all the arts, and to describe a painter's work as poetic is to relate it to the source of all inspiration.

Herbert Read

Plate 1 SWAN SONG. 1927–8

Plate 2   FALLING STARS.   1912

Plate 3   ELMS.   1914

Plate 4 THE MENIN ROAD. 1918

Plate 5 SANCTUARY WOOD, DAWN. 1917

Plate 6   CHILTERNS UNDER SNOW.   1923

Plate 7   THE POND.   1921–24

Plate 8 DYMCHURCH STEPS. 1923

Plate 9 Winter Sea. 1925–37

Plate 10 ST. PANCRAS LILIES. 1927

Plate 11   DAHLIAS.   1927

Plate 12   STILL LIFE.   1927

Plate 13   DEAD SPRING.   1928–9

Plate 14   ATLANTIC.   1931

Plate 15
THE SOUL VISITING THE MANSIONS OF THE DEAD. 1932

Plate 16 LANDSCAPE OF THE MEGALITHS. 1934

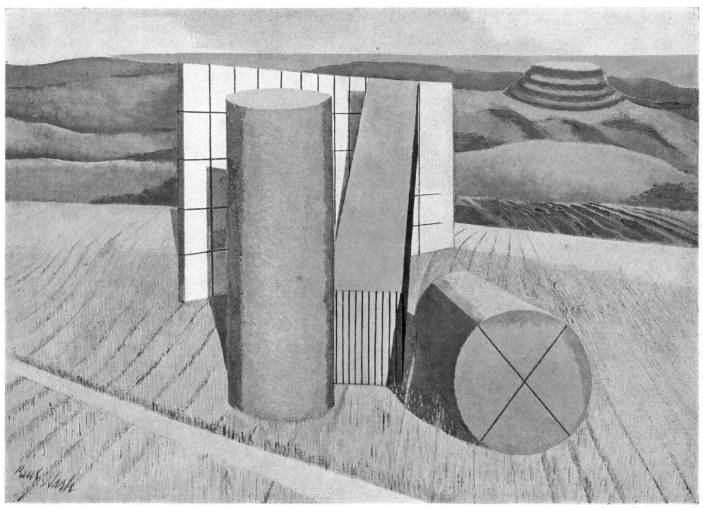

Plate 17 EQUIVALENTS FOR THE MEGALITHS. 1935

Plate 18   LANDSCAPE FROM A DREAM.   1938

Plate 19   Nostalgic Landscape.   1923–38

Plate 20   MONSTER FIELD.   1939

Plate 21 THE ARCHER. 1930–37–42

Plate 22   EARTH HOME *or* THE FORTRESS.   1939

Plate 23 Grotto in Snow. 1938–9

Plate 24   MOONLIGHT VOYAGE: FLYING AGAINST GERMANY.   1940

Plate 25 HAMPDENS AT SUNSET. 1940

Plate 26 LEBENSRAUM. 1939

Plate 27 TOTES MEER, DEAD SEA. 1940–41

Plate 28 NORTHERN ADVENTURE. 1929–41

Plate 29 BATTLE OF BRITAIN. 1941

Plate 30   Madamite Moon.   1941

Plate 31 SUNFLOWER AND SUN. 1943

Plate 32 PILLAR AND MOON. 1932–42